# Preserving the Unraveled

*poems by*

# Katharine Cristiani

*Finishing Line Press*
Georgetown, Kentucky

# Preserving the Unraveled

## ACKNOWLEDGMENTS

Thanks to the editors of the following journals for previously publishing the
following poems, sometimes slightly different version or with different titles:

*Sky Island Journal*—"No Lemons, No Preserves"
*Fahmidan Journal*—"When they ask, How's your mother? I cannot say"
*Full House Literary Magazine*—"In Search of a Ladder"
*San Pedro Review*—"Storm Warnings"
*Willows Wept Review*—"I Collect Scars" and "Tide and Current Almanac:
Circumnavigating Adulthood"

Publisher: Leah Huete de Maines
Editor: Christen Kincaid
Cover Art: Katharine Cristiani
Author Photo: Bethany Holmes
Cover Design: Elizabeth Maines McCleavy

Order online: www.finishinglinepress.com
also available on amazon.com

Author inquiries and mail orders:
Finishing Line Press
PO Box 1626
Georgetown, Kentucky 40324
USA

# Contents

## Storm Warnings

I long for corn fields, the freedom
to count the moments before rain hits
     somersaulting clouds
          a curtain of dark gray marching
          a tempo to run to
          a door open
               my mother's head tilted,
               fingers curled like her father's
               who never learned to read a book but
               read the sky for sustenance.

You cannot seek shelter
if you do not feel the weather coming.
City cell phones pierce
a warning, digital
disconnected from wind
               late.
The storm hit
     snuck in
     flooded
row homes, train tracks
sliced by power lines
disfigured black umbrellas tumble
across asphalt streams.

I do not bother with an umbrella.   I prefer
rain to drip    from eyelashes, encase skin
                   I trust
         my thumb joint to ache
     my knee to sigh
my body to shepherd me to shelter. I should be
too young to feel the weather
but my heels are rooted
             I smell soil.

## My Mother Did Not Sew

She grilled with an umbrella
in the eye of a storm. She seared steak rare,
drank beer in cans wrapped in koozies,
wrapped us in wooden shutters,
the glow of her cackle
turned hurricanes into candlelight.

She did not sit with her back to the door.
She did whistle loudly across grocery store aisles
to call her chicks home to roost.

She shared her chest graciously, boobs
more comfortable than a pillow, she'd say.
My head on her chest, a place
                    to rest
                    to run to
                    to call on Sundays,
always a drive in the sunshine, top down
or a hailstorm knocking at the roof.

Either way the Missouri and Mississippi Rivers meet
          rise and fall
          green to muddy.
Either way, she floated with the current
                    stargazed in awe of heat lightning.

## Love for a Sago Palm

My roots dangle, drag on city streets—asphalt, broken sidewalks, charcoal air. I am without land. I shepherd the sago palm of my ancestors, buckle it in the front seat, drive east on I-70.

•

I wonder when my great grandmother planted the palm pup in Laredo, did she know the smell of handmade tortillas was enough to feed it for generations? Did she sit on her porch, fan in her hand and watch it sprout?

When my eighteen-year-old grandmother was sent off with a family secret, did she pot the plant, a friend to hold in the back alley? Did its blades soften into a handkerchief, dry her sweat?

Secret soaked in soil, she put on her face, married, settled down, lounged on a concrete patio—sago palm, cucumbers, magnolia.

•

It was time. My father carried the weight of roots crowded in clay up the Mississippi to seasons. This plant was not made for the Midwest. Too wet, too cold, risk root rot or death by winter.

Yet he had faith it could survive the crossing of seasons. He laid it in the family plot, tended to the palm like a horse on his farm, apple in hand, blanket to weather the winter.

Each year, boots laced, my father crunched through snow, fed cardinals plump, waited for the pups to rise. He harvested them, raised the family.

•

His grandchild was born, tiny hands to clasp his finger through the first round of chemo. He taught her to hold a shovel, dig dirt.

•

Four years later, in the shorter days of sepia tone, the sago palm witnessed
        my father
                    shake his head,
                    remove his oxygen tube,
                    settle into his recliner.

It heard him whisper, *Take care of the plants.*

**In Search of a Ladder**

My hands are full
of groceries
bills and the regular things—
a young child, a sixty-hour job
a cat that pees where she wishes.
My hands are full
of Alzheimer's Disease, decisions
delusions
power of attorney
seventeen pages of times new roman font
a manilla envelope full of manuals
origami creases in translucent paper
tiny translations in so many languages
      I cannot find my own
      *how to build the dresser that is already built*
      *install a car seat outgrown, register the new now-old blender*
      *the warranty for the roof that long slid down a hill.*

I am trying.

I glance at my father's practical eyes
behind glass
      a rectangle to the garage
      a slow baseball game on the radio
      the ladder stored on its side
                  sturdy.

I am trying.

**Watching a squirrel while sitting in traffic, late to pick up my daughter**

The sun slows
she takes one bite of a tomato
leaves the rest to rot—N*ot stolen*, she swears.
*For the ants*, she swears. A groundhog catches her eye
she skitters onto a cable wire        blinks
    chases another squirrel up a tree
                        leaps to the next
            dashes
        like a New York City rat
        fat and guilty.
Her bushy tail sways
                a grandfather clock
        ticking, tocking
                like me
        chimes always late
always running
        to a meeting / appointment / pick up / drop off
        to my mother
my eyes twitch    teeth clench
head never still.

## A Hard Word to Spell

### EARLY STAGE

*What elves?* asks Mom.
> *You know,* I say, *the handmade ones.*
> *Velvet coats, cotton beards, miniature bells*
> > *on pointed shoes.*
> The ones that flew
> in our living room every Christmas
> > for the last
> > > twenty years.

> *Remember last week,* I say,
> *you explained to our friend that the fishing line*
> *above the fireplace isn't a cobweb, it's for our elves.*
> Remember the elves?

> > Remember?

Her face scolds, *No. There are no elves.*

### MIDDLE STAGE
> *How are you?*
> I know the answer.

*I am fine, I feel fine.*
*You know I'm president?*
*Your brother died.*
*He had six children, all six feet tall.*

*They are bringing the pancakes now. You should go.*
> I try, *I can stay while you eat.*

*It's the middle of the night. You should go.*
> I try, *We're both up anyway.*
> Her skin, an onion shedding brittle layers.
> She refuses to bathe.
> I try. *Let me get lotion.*

6

*I'm late to church. You should go.*
> Her toenails thick yellow witches' claws,
> black and split. Too long
> have they dug through socks,
> seeking sunlight.
> They cannot be contained
> nor voice their dissent.

> *I love you,* I say.
*I love you, too. You should go.*

### LATE STAGE—MY GRANDMOTHER
Early Christmas morning the nurse calls, *She's dying. Come now.*
That year, my grandmother had settled into the disease,
carved space to dance in stillness to Italian opera,
embraced a straw for her red velvet frozen yogurt—
she set down her spoon.

### A BLESSING
May my mother follow in the footsteps of her mother.
May she soften. May she walk upon pink sand
as the tide sweeps past her ankles.
May her toes settle into the cool heaviness
between sand and tide.

## Rough Rope

In the sinews of my flesh
        I tie a figure-eight
                double knot
                            five parallel lines
                snaked just so
        around my spine
        through my pelvis—
one tug
        & I tighten
                into a boa constrictor.
                    This knot
                holds over 300 pounds.
        I do not need
the night to hide inside of.

**Sunset over a 36 Hour Day**[1]

In this beige cube that pretends
to be an apartment, I pretend
you could be happy. You pretend
to understand what I am talking about.
You are my mother after all.
Flat gray peeks through blinds
whispers to me,
> *You pretend this isn't a prison.*

*Remember,* I say
& then remember
I shouldn't say remember.
*I was thinking about sunsets,* I say
while pretending
you are not pacing, picking skin,
tucking people's names into a suitcase.
You say, *It's been a long day. You should go.*

I remember volcanic cliffs, jagged rocks softening
to silhouettes against sunset.

Me, nestled in your chest,
your breath rising against my sunburnt cheeks.

You taught me to bow to the pink passing of time,
the quiet of sky as it purples.

After the moon lifted the silence, you promised
I would be safe, salt would hold me.

---

[1]When caring for a loved one with Alztheimer's, I recommend two guides: 1) *The 36-Hour Day: A Family Guide to Caring for People Who Have Alzheimer Disease, Other Dementias, and Memory Loss* by Nancy L. Mace and Peter V. Rabins; 2) The Alzheimer's Association and their 24-hour hotline—https://www.alz.org/

**When they ask, How's your mother? I cannot say**

Under the cloak of bark
an Emerald Ash Borer laid a maze,
                    ate the innards
devoured      her brain,
gray matter sawed      to dust
but not dust    sanded smooth
where ridges should run
                            rough and wild.

She, the tree reaching
crown to stars, roots to rocks
            buckled
at wind howling
a slow creek
            trunk split
            heart exposed
            leaves alive.

I consider saying,
*She is anxious in the fall sun.*

## When I Think of Death

I think of becoming dirt
deep black, moist
full of life—
trees become stumps      become homes
mice, mushrooms, kingfishers
holes hallowed by the rhythm of a woodpecker
    a rosewood marimba
    played with six mallets, three in each hand.

In this dance of roots, earthworms weave
pine needles and moss into a blanket, nestle
in the space between air and core.

Flames speak in deep voices of blues and purples,
coals crackles at a joke, sizzle to sleep
after one too many glasses of wine.

I wish I could open a window
let you fly out, give you the gift of dirt.

**No Lemons, No Preserves**

In 9th grade biology class
I learned the word preserved meant frogs
& with scissors I sliced skin, found stomach turned sac
lungs deflated, heart & liver in the center,
the rough slipperiness
        of gestation, of evolution
        of legs that leap, eyes that color night.

Later, I learned preserved meant survival:
salt on meat, jerked journeys
across swamps North to escape chains & cotton
across deserts West when land was dry then repossessed
        —fingers bled.

Even later, I tasted preserved lemons
        sweet sour salty sunshine
slimy, like the frog, but bright with flavor.

I long for preservation
for my mother's mind:
        vivacious
        waving to water, listening to shore.

But psychiatric drugs are not lemon water,
no slice of sunshine or rind that binds a thing whole.
Today decays into tomorrow into next year
        a slow slipping
            an endless sun setting
                into fog.

**Preserving the Unraveled**

Stowed in my closet,
twelve spools of quiet
colors, needles thick, thin
useful
except
I do not mend, I collect
          scars, skin, sunsets.

My sweaters unravel,
buttons dangle off shirts
blue threads
                    hanging
twist in wind, tangle into dawn,
          break
                    into the beak of a yellow finch
who tethers thin twigs & dead leaves,
          builds a home.

Where strands of spring light peep through nest,
I wander into rain
          turn over a rock,
          seek earthworms.

## Touchstones

We are safe
until T-boned.
First thought: you have got
to fucking be kidding me—
not        another        thing.
Then:
            silence
broken
            my daughter's cry—
she is ok.

I must be ok. I am always
ok. I am rock embedded in creek,
etched with fossils. I do not crack.

Over millennia, mountains
soften creek beds into inviting steps.

I skip a stone
            to erase the Xs on my knee,
                        the Hs on my hip socket.
                                    I can't make it all the way.
I breathe, build a cairn
                        and keep
                                    skipping.

## At Junctures

Stretched rubber bands
   hold my limbs in place
   so tight      they may
break
      or disintegrate
as old rubber bands do—
   no longer useful.

I want to my body to be useful—
to walk
with rubber bands fresh from a head of broccoli
chase away shadows like my cat at the wall
sit upright at the dinner table
stand so feet remember weight
dance.

## I Settled on Jade

on smokey smooth green, a touchstone to rub between fingers,
slide up and down a chain. I considered smudging sage, piling
oranges in bowls or unearthing my grandmother's rosary but
                          the jade necklace hung steady.
It grew into me as vines do, bathed me, cradled my neck at night
until the chain broke,
            rolled the stone across the bathroom tile.
                          It was then I wished for a pocket.

**Break: a transitive verb**

I am breaking; you are broken

i.  There is nothing fragile about broken glass—
sharp shards of crystal wine glass shattered,
the dense puzzle of a mason jar dropped onto stone,
cubes of pyrex exploded over the kitchen stove.
I swallowed one in soup. The doctor said, *eat yogurt*.

ii.  After the last frost, after spring storms
extract roots of giants, we break rocky soil.
In holes smaller than my pinky, we plant seeds,
                                        kale and lettuce.

iii.  Fallen branches, two inches thick
are best broken by a child,
a whack against a tree. They crack
in two      fly
                        this break is playing—
                sticks, pine needles, ferns
                        the building of a fort.

## Ecdysis

I cup my hands into the creek
out of fear of all that is parched,
      trout cold water
               drips,
        I am not a chalice
or even a mason jar.

Hands wet, I touch river rock,
borrow heat like a snake sunning
               into tomorrow.

              I shed my skin
not the metamorphosis of a monarch,
the inevitable wrinkle
      of one foot    in front of the other
        the slip
          of one day into the next.

I collect the remains
      brittle    destined to crack,
lay them gently in a shoebox.
Maybe this old skin will fit again    or maybe
I will cut it into cloth, stitch snakeskin boots.

## Dance Through Decades

They did not tell me my body would change.
I'm not talking about puberty, but hips settling into a saddle
tasked with carrying weight
until the saddle needs repair or the trail ride ends.

They did not tell me the next decade
would be an iron
hot and wanting. I am branded
   sunspots, spider veins
     tequila sunrise smeared to storm clouds under eyes.

They did not tell me my etched body,
fine lines chiseled by touch, by unhindered motion
would stumble
                into an ungraceful dance.

Tonight, I slip into the silk of a night lake,
my body arches into a bow, dives as an arrow
                unfurls moonlight.

## Alone in the Woods in my 40s

I have a tick on my outer eyelid.          Grateful
for a rearview mirror, for tweezers          confounded
upon realizing I cannot wear reading glasses while removing it.

My eyesight was perfect.
The prism I got for my fifth birthday
          danced
                    refracted rainbows
but these two panes of glass are flat.

I look up          green smear
where a field of clover should lie.          Confused
I consider an article: Lyme disease
could be mitigated by removing
certain non-native ornamental plants
revered for their white prolific blossoms.
This seems simple enough.    Easier
than steading my hand.
                         One eye closed
I stare at the black blob
                    capable of drawing a bullseye
                                        of playing darts.
I consider urgent care
               but settle on grace—
                    a small butterfly    orange resting on breeze
                    soft metal between fingers
                    my firm surgical wiggle
                                        satisfied
          to pluck something substantial    alive
          I tug    extract the tick          intact.

## In Remembrance of the Balance Brace

> *"In the balance brace maneuver, the kayak is held at the*
> *capsize point indefinitely—without ever going over—using*
> *the flotation of the upper body and Greenland-style paddle.*
> *It's almost as relaxing as a break on shore."*
> —Paddler Magazine

After the surrender,
the moment my body draped
into the ocean, trusted tension,
my shoulders swept magic across the surface
     water made solid
          our bodies
          boats
          blades
     our disbelief
          suspended        on its side.


We awoke to orange juice. Hand squeezed,
the street vendor's cart overflowing
with a sunrise that would soon wash out the madrugada
     the twenty moments cupped in indigo
     when backs of hands brush lightly,
     yawn upon twisted sheets.

Cómo amaneciste? How did you dawn?

## TIDE AND CURRENT ALMANAC: Circumnavigating Adulthood

The only shade to be found
on the islands of the Sea of Cortez
is inside a cliff. I nap in rock.

The water calm, clear.
The salt thick.

Fresh water was sparse.
I was thirsty        until not.

Waves want to come in sets of seven,
crash deep gray under a storm,
sheets of rain racing.

The tide obeys,
defies, obeys,
defies the timeless science;
fickle wind, the evolving contours
of my loss.
The tide recedes
            until it doesn't.

Twice a month the full moon
pulls the tide, gives permission
to the currents to rip
the ocean into rivers rushing.

From the seat of a sharp rock
I bear witness
to the twenty-minute miracle
of slack tide:
the racing
    slows
        stops
        is still
            until it isn't.

## With Thanks

I want to appreciate: Judith Lagana for her mentorship, editing and loving pushes—without her I would have never considered publication; Marjorie Stelmach, who believed in me as a teenager and unveiled the galaxy of poetry; Deepam Wadds, for creating a loving writing community; Cynthia Stretch, Steve Mathews, Rasma Haidri and Barbara Krasner for reading and commenting on many of these poems.

I have yet to find words to express my deep gratitude for my mom and dad, Therese and Michael Cristiani. They built a strong foundation for me to stand on, pointed to the stars, and encouraged me to wander through the wonder of the world with confidence and empathy.

I am beyond grateful for my chosen family. Without their love and support over the last several years, I would have been left unraveled or perhaps pickled. Thank you to MK, TB, RNS, RW, GH, JC, AR, JK, JMA, JH, SM and CS along with my entire union family. I love you all.

Thank you to SK for filling my heart each day—I love you to the moon and back.

**Katharine Cristiani** is a mother, union organizer and poet who calls Philadelphia home. After college, she put down her pen for twenty years. Encouraged by loved ones, she embraced a period of physical recovery to rediscover her voice in poetry. Her work appears in *San Pedro Review, Literary Mama, Willows Wept Review, Full House Literary Magazine, Neologism Poetry Journal, Sky Island Journal* and elsewhere.

Katharine is devoted to building a multi-racial, multi-gendered working-class movement powerful enough to reconstruct our beautiful, messy world into one that values life and love over profit. With roots in the Midwest, she loves both the quiet of cornfields and vibrant, gritty cities. She builds campfires in any weather with love and prowess.

www.ingramcontent.com/pod-product-compliance
Lightning Source LLC
Chambersburg PA
CBHW022107080426
42734CB00009B/1505